A Time to Grow

Books by the Authors

A Time to Grow

Gladis & Gordon DePree

Illustrations by Martha Bentley

ZONDERVAN PUBLISHING HOUSE
OF THE ZONDERVAN CORPORATION
GRAND RAPIDS, MICHIGAN 49506

A Time to Grow
Copyright © 1981 by the Zondervan Corporation

This printing May 1981

Library of Congress Cataloging in Publication Data
DePree, Gladis, 1933–
    A time to grow.

    1. Meditations. I. DePree, Gordon. II. Title.
BV4832.2.D449   242'.2   81-1464
ISBN 0-310-23681-9   AACR2

Scripture passages are from the Jerusalem Bible, copyright
1966 by Barton, Longman & Todd, Ltd. and Doubleday &
Company, Inc.

Edited by Mary Bombara
Design by Mary Bombara and Martha Bentley

Printed in the United States of America

This is the season for which all other seasons pass. It is the time of the full green leaf, the red tomato, the ripe soft corn, the fruit in clusters. It is the season of now. No more hiding in the seed nor shy peeping buds; the sun is on us, and what we would become has found its moment. This is the season . . . this is

A TIME TO GROW.

*"Your achievements are the measure
of your power."*
Psalm 66:3

1

THE ACHIEVEMENTS of God the creator are
astounding . . . and as his creatures we each
have in the heart of us a tiny echo of God,
the need to achieve.

It was a great moment the first time we
discovered we could whistle a tune, or tie our
own shoes, or pass a finger through a candle
flame without getting burned. And then there
were days when it was hard to whistle, there
were knots more difficult to tie and untie, and
flames that were not so easy to pass through
without getting burned. . . . But we learned
how; and each time we did it, there was that
feeling of achievement, that sense of being
more truly alive.

Now, all through life we keep encountering
these knots and flames, and each time we
achieve the mastery of them there is again in
us that tiny echo of God, who looked at all
he had created and done and saw that it was
very good.

*"What is expected of stewards is that
each one should be found worthy of
his trust."*
1 Corinthians 4:2

CHOOSING A CAREER as a young person,
changing careers in mid-life, finding satisfying
work after the children are grown, fulfilling
the need to be active as a separate person
while the children are small. . . . All these are
deeply perplexing choices—choices that
cause us to look into ourselves, to ask,
"What is the special ability that has been
given to me? Who can tell me?"

The stewardship of our lives is a private
transaction between our maker and us. Only
we can feel that vital contact point, that
source of deep aliveness at the quick of our
being where time stands still and we are in
the flow of God. That is *our* unique trust.
And once we discover it, all that is required is
that we use it. To use our gifts is to be found
worthy of them. One might even say that
trusting in God is returning his trust in us.

*". . . by his power fulfil all your desires
for goodness and complete all that you
have been doing through faith. . . ."*
2 Thessalonians 1:11

3

SOMETIMES I KNOW what I would like to be and
I feel the whole of my self responding to joy
and beauty, to an inner vision of life that is
filled with light and power, with truth and
honest-to-God integrity. I see life clearly and
want to share it. . . .

But where is the market for dreams? The
whole earth is caught up in the scramble for
survival and people buy only what they
need. In a world busy with the rush for soap
and toothpaste, new cars and pudding mixes,
who will buy dreams? Perhaps I must learn to
repackage my dreams. . . . Yet I must take
care that they are not lost in the packaging. If
in my work I keep in touch with my dreams,
whatever I do to contribute to the world's
survival will take on that quality of truth and
power and honest-to-God integrity that I
cherish so deeply.

"In the morning sow your seed, do not let your hands lie idle in the evening. For which will prove successful, this or that, you cannot tell; and it may be that both will turn out well together."
Ecclesiastes 11:6

4

THE GREAT RUSH of God's power flows into each of us. We do not always know how it will best be expressed in us and sometimes hesitate, casting about for the most valid statement of this power in and through our lives.

Hesitation that is discernment is good, but constant hesitation is crippling. Jump in and try! Sow your fields in the morning and write your poems at night. Go to work to earn your bread at noon and dream your dreams at midnight. The variety of expression we are given as containers of the power of God is endless. If we live with vigor and sensitivity, we will find that God is there. The only person who will be left out, who will stand sadly at life's end, is the person who was so afraid of doing the wrong thing that he or she never did anything at all.

"People who long to be rich are a prey to temptation; they get trapped into all sorts of foolish and dangerous ambitions which eventually plunge them into ruin and destruction."
1 Timothy 6:9

WHAT I DO or do not have in this world has little to do with the worth of my soul, but how I go about acquiring possessions has a great deal to do with the quality of my life.

If I set my goals on having rather than on being, a subtle transformation takes place in me. Days seem to shrink into meaningless stretches as they point toward a time when I either will or will not have what I want. People seem less important if they do not directly concern what I am trying to get, and as a result, my life becomes a narrow channel between myself and the object of my desire. Having robbed myself of true friends, time, and spontaneous enjoyment of life, I find I have become isolated and lonely, cynical, and full of fear. Is what I want worth all this?

"My flesh has bloomed again."
Psalm 28:7

THERE IS SOMETHING about a plant struggling to keep alive in a clay pot that I identify with very deeply. I will water it and move it from sun to shade and handle it as gently as if its survival were somehow tied to mine.

Perhaps it is. The life-power in a plant comes from the same source that my life-power comes from—God. And when I am down and withered, like a dry stalk in an old clay pot, I hope God will treat me gently, give me sun and water, and let me bloom again. In my dryest, brownest moments, it is reassuring to know that somewhere in me there is still the power to bloom.

*"For your part, if you walk before me
with innocence of heart and honesty
. . . I will make [you] . . . secure."*
1 Kings 9:4–5

7

AN HONEST, open-hearted attitude toward
God, life, and people will make me a secure
person. This is not just a promise, it is a
natural consequence.

Most of our insecurities arise from a state of
double-mindedness within ourselves. We
admire words like innocence and honesty,
and yet we are afraid to be identified with
them. Both of these words carry with them
the connotation of not knowing the score.
Innocence is aligned with stupidity. Honesty
is for the ignorant man who knowingly cuts
himself out of a lot of benefits he could have,
if. . . . And while deep in our spirits we
dream of being innocent and honest, our
sense of false pride pulls us into being
complex and conniving. It is the disparity
between our inner and outer vision that gives
us a sickening sense of doom.

If I ever become mature and stable enough
to value my connection with God above all
else, I will be able to make *"honesty and
innocence"* look so good that people will be
dying to have it.

*"Make the preaching of the Good
News your life's work. . . ."*
2 Timothy 4:5

"LIFE'S WORK" has an exciting ring to it. It
calls to mind great artists or statesmen,
persons who had a cohesive purpose to the
living of their days. All the obstacles, the
trouble, the toil, and even temporary failures,
only give the story zest when one has a life's
work.

In today's mobile society, with its job
obsolescence and changing markets, having
a life's work becomes increasingly difficult.
Yet, for the follower of Jesus Christ, if living
out the Good News is his life's basic purpose,
there is continuity in spite of constant
change. He can move from place to place
and change from job to job without ever
interrupting his basic occupation—sharing
God's love.

*"But God loved us with so much love
that he was generous with his mercy."
Ephesians 2:4*

MERCY, THE QUALITY of being able to feel the
pain and need of the other person, is very
often tied to the ability to love.

If I love you, I will feel your need to search,
your compulsion to prove yourself, and will
know why you have done what you have
done, even though it was not wise. I will
even be able to feel your regret (with you)
when you are foolish. If I love you, I will
have the generosity to overlook your faults
and encourage your good points. I will be
giving far past the point where I should
logically have stopped. I will always suppose
that what was wrong will be forgotten in a
tomorrow where we will all be a little wiser. If
I love you, without demanding a price for it, I
will find my world has become, surprisingly,
not a poorer place, but a larger, richer,
warmer place to be. Blessed are the merciful,
for they will know the loving presence of
God who is generous with his mercy.

*"Happy the man whom Yahweh
accuses of no guilt, whose spirit is
incapable of deceit."*
Psalm 32:2

10

LIFE IS NOT divided between those who do
wrong and those who do no wrong, but
between those who see and admit their faults
and those who do not. Being blind to one's
own faults ends in blaming everyone else
when things go wrong. When others must
bear all the blame and I am the only faultless
one, the company gets rather sparse.

In the tangled interrelationships of our lives,
none of us escapes without fault. The only
person who remains free is the one who
admits he is a part of the whole human scene
and assumes his share of the blame, asking
for forgiveness wherever it is needed to clear
the air and make a fresh start.

"Do not stay away from the meeting of the community . . . but encourage each other to go."
Hebrews 10:25

11

A SENSE OF community is vital to the human spirit. I may live in a large impersonal city where my neighbors exist behind locked doors, or out in the country where there is not another house for as far as I can see. . . . But if I have a place where I can meet with others in a common spirit, I have a community.

In the company of other believers, I find God speaking to me through many voices and smiling at me through many faces. The sight of busy responsible people kneeling in prayer affirms in my mind that God is a part of the ongoing life of the world. Standing with a cup of coffee after the church service and sharing hopes and dreams, and sometimes disappointments, with others affirms my belief that God really cares. And in the love I share with others in the community, I come to know in a special way what it means that God is love. If I absent myself from such vital community, I am the loser.

*"Do not be stubborn when the cause
is not a good one."*
Ecclesiastes 8:3

12

STUBBORNNESS IS THE flip side of the coin of
steadfastness. The problem with this coin is
knowing which side is heads and which side
is tails.

Standing for principles is good. Nagging
about details is destructive. Holding on to
values is commendable. Holding on to values
which alienate people from one another is
questionable. Standing for the keeping of
rules is firmness. Keeping these rules blindly
is insensitivity. Stubbornness can make us so
long-wearing that we outlive our usefulness.
It is a blessing and a curse, a strength and a
weakness. It keeps us holding on . . . long
after we should have let go.

Stubbornness or steadfastness? Perhaps this
coin is only safe when it is flipped by the
hand of love.

*"Offer them bread and water for them
to eat and drink, and let them go back
to their master . . . raiding parties
never invaded the territory of Israel
again."*
2 Kings 6:22–23

13

WHEN SOMEONE infringes on my rights,
invades my territory, and outrages my sense
of justice, what do I do? Do I strike back,
paying cut for cut, line for line, argument for
argument?

I can do this if I want to be fighting for the
rest of my life. I may even beat my opponent
to the ground and ride off in victory . . .
leaving a smoldering enemy behind who will
get me at the first opportunity. But if I decide
that my life is going to amount to more than
one battle after another, if I honestly have
more important things to do than fight, I can
step in and stop the whole process. I can
repay hostility with gentleness, aggression
with agreement, and invasion with
hospitality. An enemy who is taken in and
fed and watered suffers from such chagrin
that he never dares show his face again. Or if
he does, it becomes the face of a friend.

"I agree that there are no forbidden things for me, but I am not going to let anything dominate me."
1 Corinthians 6:12

14

LIFE IS extremely complex. Good things such as optimism and hope for the future keep us alive—but at the same time they can sap the life out of us for today.

It is not wrong to plan and dream and hope, but if I do it in the place of actualizing and acting and fulfilling, it is not right. I can get stretched so thin in my grasp toward the future that I come apart in the present. I want this, I want that, I hope for this job and letter and contract and opening . . . and while I beat a path to the mailbox I stumble over daily miracles and kick them aside.

Oh, God! Help me to let go of the future and live now. One of these days the future is going to come and I might miss it, thinking it's just another one of those ordinary days. Help me to let go, and the future will lose its stranglehold on me.

"My prayer is undefiled."
Job 16:17

15

WE THINK OF prayers as very holy things. Yet anything that we hold as unquestionably holy can become empty, if that thing is less than God himself.

Prayer can become a vain exercise in which we love to hear the sound of our own voices. It can be an endless chain of platitudes with which we bore ourselves senseless. It can be the result of social pressure within a given group, to pray a certain way, to say certain phrases. It can be miles of printed prayers in prayer books and liturgies which roll over our tongues and never once enter our minds or hearts. Prayer may be the desperate attempt of the straying spirit to twist God's arm, to tempt God to bless that which is not able to be blessed. . . .

The most profound prayers we will ever utter may be the ones in which we have come to the end of ourselves, painful as that may be, and have nothing to say but, *"Oh, God!"*

*". . . opportunities for announcing the
message and proclaiming the mystery
of Christ."*
Colossians 4:3

16

THE GOOD NEWS of Jesus Christ is both a
message and a mystery. The message
consists of words that can be spoken. *God is
love.* These words are easy to say, both to
ourselves and to others.

But mystery is more subtle. It is solved by
discovering clues and following them. Christ
gave us clues. *The first shall be last. The
giver will be the receiver. Those who are
willing to lay down their lives will know what
it is to live. Blessed are the meek, for they
shall inherit the earth.*

All of these sound like parts of a giant puzzle,
until we follow each clue to its farthest limit.
Then, and only then, will we begin to
comprehend what it is all about. Some things
can be spoken. Other things must be lived to
be believed . . . to be shared.

"Anyone who does not look after his own [family] . . . has rejected the faith and is worse than an unbeliever."
1 Timothy 5:8

17

BELIEVING IN GOD makes us aware of our connection to other people. When a family tension arises, or there is unsuitable behavior within the family, we cannot simply cut ourselves off. We *are* related, both to one another and to God.

Once we accept this unalterable fact, what we do within this given framework makes the difference between creative or destructive family patterns. Again, our faith can give us perspective. As God is patient with us, so we are to be patient with others. God gives to us, even though we sometimes forget to thank him. He forgives, no matter how many times we offend him. In our relationship to God, we find not only the responsibility of family patterns, but the example of how to live them out wisely.

"Everyone has his own burden to carry."
Galatians 6:5

"You should carry each other's troubles and fulfil the law of Christ."
Galatians 6:2

18

SOME DAYS when I walk down the street, I feel a sense of heaviness pressing on me, a feeling of delayed hopes, frustrated dreams, uncertain futures . . . an unnamed sense of dread. Everyone else seems to be hurrying along, carefree, coming, going, buying, and selling. . . .

But if I stop to look closely at a single face—perhaps the face of the person waiting next to me at the counter—I can see the same emotions playing across his face, perhaps for different reasons, or reasons even more real than mine. Everyone seems to be caught in his own private web of troubles and worries. The only time it ever seems lighter is when one human being reaches out and lifts another's load.

The spirit of Jesus Christ within us can give us that sensitivity and compassion.

"What the Spirit brings is . . . love, joy, peace, patience, kindness, goodness, trustfulness, gentleness and self-control."
Galatians 5:22

19

IF WE COULD be filled with the Spirit of God, we would be the most heavenly people on earth.

Imagine being filled with love and joy and peace, and having the patience to bear with people who are filled with hate and anger and turmoil. Imagine being filled with kindness and goodness to such an extent that we could be able to trust those who have let us down, again and again. Imagine being gentle and generous with others, and using that hawklike eye on ourselves in a self-control that is unrelenting. Imagine!

We do not need to imagine. We could experience it, if we would.

*"To many I have seemed an enigma,
but you are my firm refuge."*
Psalm 71:7

To SOME, the Christian lifestyle may seem
puzzling. The followers of Jesus Christ claim
to be free, and yet they are bound by some
of the strongest standards in the world. There
is a stability about them, and yet they go
wandering over the earth like strangers and
pilgrims, sharing the good news of Christ in
places where no sensible person would want
to go. What is the basis of this strange
contradiction?

The enigmatic quality of the Christian lifestyle
comes from an inner strength. We are free,
but only within the bounds of God's love.
We are stable because the earth is the
Lord's, and everywhere we go is home. . . .
But we wander about because creation is still
at work in us, bringing the world to be. Our
inner strength comes from being anchored in
God . . . but with enough rope to float with
the tide.

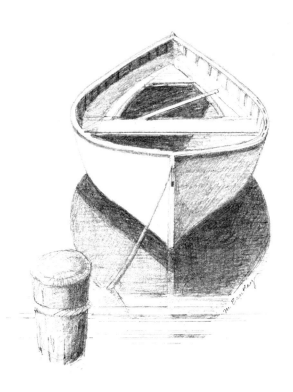

"Bless Yahweh . . . remember all his kindnesses . . . in crowning you with love and tenderness."
Psalm 103:1, 2, 4

21

WE ARE ALL, at one time or another, afraid of being taken advantage of. The nicer we are, the more people push us around. The natural reaction is to stiffen up, to show the world. . . .

And then, midway through the toughness pose, we sense the futility of it all. God, who is the ultimate power in this world, crowns his actions with love and tenderness. His tenderness to us is the mark of his strength. He could destroy us all like an ant hill, with one swoop of his hand . . . and instead, he patiently gentles us along all our lives, knowing why we do what we do and understanding that when we bare our teeth to bite, it is probably out of desperation. He gentles us through our hostile moments until we can smile again.

Like the gentleness of God, our gentleness is the mark of our strength.

"Do all that has to be done without complaining or arguing and then you will be innocent and genuine. . . ."
Philippians 2:14–15

WHEN I COMPLAIN, I am out of touch with myself. When I argue, I am out of touch with others. A complaint is really an accusation against myself, an admission that I cannot cope with my environment or change to accommodate it. An argument is a desperate attempt to throw the blame for the whole situation on another person, a last ditch effort to prove that even though I am miserable, I am right.

As a follower of Jesus Christ, I can be in touch with myself and with other people. There is no need to complain, because whatever the circumstances are I can take them. There is no need to argue, because I do not need to be right. I am learning and I could be wrong. The pressure is off, and I, the schemer and the phony, can now be me, the innocent and the genuine . . . and not even mind if these are laugh-words in a world that is out of touch with itself.

"To the rock too high for me, lead me."
Psalm 61:2

23

SOMETHING THAT IS too high for me suggests the need to stretch and grow, like a child standing on tiptoe to touch the top of a chest of drawers. Growing demands aims, goals, and ideas that I am not able to grasp . . . yet.

God, give me ideas that I can't easily cope with or dismiss. Give me work to do that is too difficult, that taxes every part of my mind and heart. Let me jump into life over my head. Let me always be climbing toward the part of the mountain that I can barely glimpse, and that only on a sunny day. Keep leading me to a life that is too big, too good, too high. Keep stretching me so that some day I may stand tall in your sight.

"He is like a tree by the waterside that thrusts its roots to the stream: when the heat comes it feels no alarm, its foliage stays green."
Jeremiah 17:8

THERE ARE DAYS when the heat is on us, and life *does* seem more like a choice of nightmares than the dream we had hoped it would be. Is the dream gone? Which compromise should we make? Which lesser thing should we choose?

And then we send down that taproot to the living source and are reaffirmed. God *is,* and God is a positive ruling force in the world. When confronted with a choice of nightmares, we have a third option. . . . We can turn away and say, *"No, thanks, I won't have either of them, because I believe life is good. I will not settle for any form of evil or destructiveness."*

When our roots are in God, that refreshing living water gives us hidden strength!

*"Let earth praise Yahweh:
sea-monsters and all the deeps, fire
and hail, snow and mist, gales that
obey his decree. . . ."*
Psalm 148:7–8

OFTEN OUR BELIEFS are not strong enough to
sustain us in this world because we cast God
and our fears in two separate camps. All that
we are afraid of—the dark formless monsters
of our imagination, the deep waters of
despair that wash over us, the heat and
pounding that are the hail and fire of doubt,
the fierce winds of change that blow us from
our secure positions to God-knows-where-
it-will-all-end—all of this we think of as a set
of circumstances through which God must
defend and protect us, and sometimes he
does not.

But if we dare to hold these things up before
God and thank him for them, what a new
and startling light is beamed on them! They
were a part of the creative process at work in
us, and we did not recognize it.

"A servant of the Lord is not to engage in quarrels, but has to be kind to everyone, a good teacher, and patient."
2 Timothy 2:24

QUARRELS ALWAYS STEM from our weakness, from our necessity to prove that we are right especially when we are not sure about it ourselves. Cutting the other person down to our size makes him or her easier to handle.

But the follower of Jesus Christ is not engaged in the business of cutting other people down. If an opinion must be stated, it can be done in a kind, straightforward, convincing way that will build everyone up, make everyone feel a little taller, a little stronger. The words we contribute do not need to prove us right since they do not come from us. We are loving servants, bringing God's words to a world that needs them—that needs love.

"Yahweh, your memory is always fresh!"
Psalm 135:13

27

I'M NOT ALWAYS aware of the presence of God. There are sometimes whole stretches of the day when I never think of God once, consciously. Out of sight is out of mind. . . .

But I'm always aware of the presence of people. They are there, needing to be fed or listened to or met with or written to. People around me share my excitement, my disappointments, my depressions, and my joys. We are always interacting, and the moment something of significance happens (or doesn't happen), I seek out a friend to share it with. When days or months or sections of my life are past, I think of those friends in terms of what we have shared . . . what we have laughed and cried about, together.

And in a way I suppose that is how we best remember God, recalling the high points or low points when we have vitally interacted with him. Like a good friend, he was there when we needed him.

*"Let us offer God an unending
sacrifice of praise, a verbal sacrifice
that is offered everytime we
acknowledge his name."*
Hebrews 13:15

I AM THINKING about a situation which tempts
me to be bitter. I will sacrifice that desire to
be bitter and instead thank God for the
experience, for all it has taught me, for new
awarenesses, for sharpened perceptions, and
new wisdom. I have held up my bitterness
before God, and he has given *me a heart full
of blessings* in its place.

Praise, the ability to take whatever life brings
us and thank God for it, is a marvelous
release. If I do not need to be bitter about
hurts and disappointments, I get other people
and their misbehavior off my back. I can be
free because I am busy thanking God for
showing me how *not* to be in my
relationships with other people. I have
learned! I am free! I am thankful!

"We are certainly determined to behave honourably in everything we do."
Hebrews 13:18

THERE IS AN AIR of nobility about a life that is deeply honorable. A sense of honor that goes down deep into the heart of the person gives him or her an air of distinction. This is not why one should be honorable, of course. Honor is not something to be worn like a hat, to enhance the wearer, but a spirit that springs from deep within.

A life that is honorable is one which consistently chooses the best paths. It does not compromise with dishonor. It meets life wide-eyed, clear-headed, knowing and sensing and seeing all sides of a problem, empathizing with those who are caught in dishonor, never acting a cut above, yet at heart not a part of anything that would sully the spirit. To be determined to behave honorably is a lifelong occupation. It requires a daily, hourly choice and never ends. Although our determination is to behave honorably, we can never, in our human weakness, relax and say, "Now I am honorable." Honor is always a state of becoming.

*"Your words set right whoever
wavered, and strengthened every
failing knee . . . and . . . now it touches
you and you are overwhelmed."*
Job 4:4

THERE ARE NO troubles so easy to solve as the
troubles of others. I can analyze them,
theorize about them, and come to sensible,
brilliant conclusions . . . and yet the whole
time I am doing so, I have the uncomfortable
feeling that I might not be so efficient if the
problem were my own. What would I do if
my life fell apart?

And then it does. The pain, the
disillusionment, the despair. The feeling that
all my dreams have lost their tang, and
nothing means anything . . . it touches me.

Yes, I'm overwhelmed. But in some ways,
I'm grateful to be overwhelmed, thankful to
be touching base with life, even in my
capacity to suffer. I'm real. I know what it
means to descend into hell. I can learn what
it means to rise again.

"We were hoping for peace—no good came of it! For the moment of cure—nothing but terror!"
Jeremiah 14:19

31

THERE IS NOTHING quite so distressing as planning a family event—a party, a camping trip, or a summer vacation—and having it turn out to be a family war. What was meant to be a time of peace somehow turns out to be a disaster. How does this happen? Most such disasters occur when the individuals involved all have differing opinions about their *rights* in the situation. I demand my rights, stating my views, wishes, and opinions, and everyone else does the same. We end up having six different lists of rights, wishes, needs, and opinions!

But if just one person will be different, will begin to act responsibly and with imagination, trying to please someone else, bringing in a little bouquet of flowers or making a batch of someone else's favorite cookies . . . what a difference! Peace is one of those things that can't be hoped for unless we're willing to give a little.

"I call on God the Most High, on God
who has done everything for me."
Psalm 57:2

THERE ARE TWO WAYS to look at life: to
question why God is doing this *to* me, or to
believe that God is doing this *for* me.

If I can believe, unshakably, that God is *for*
me, I can have an astounding amount of
optimism. I can dare to do things that I feel
are right but have no guaranteed outcome.
Within the bounds of responsible
personhood, I can dare to choose the
creative over the safe, the dangerous over
the secure, the risk-filled over the mundane.
If God, through the events of my life, is
moving *for* me, there is no time to look back
and wonder if it was right. Life is moving,
and I must stay in the flow. Right is always
ahead.

WHEN ONE OF the power lines is down in a town, it may affect the whole system. One cut line can have far-reaching effects.

Love for one another as husband and wife . . . love as parents and children . . . love as members of an extended family . . . love as friends . . . love for one another as members of the human race. . . . The Christian faith has love as its premise. God is love. We love. But this ideal can lose its power if one of the love-lines is broken. The broken connection becomes a short circuit, and the love energy I need to keep the whole system going is wasted on one destructive relationship. If I have a love energy crisis, perhaps I should check all of my lines, and see if they're in good order.

*"As Yahweh lives, what Yahweh says
to me, that will I utter!"*
1 Kings 22:14

THE PROPHET MICAIAH was in a hot spot. There
were four hundred prophets, all telling the
king exactly what he wanted to hear . . . and
then there stood this one lone prophet,
contradicting them. His knees must have felt
like jelly when he stood up and said, "As
Yahweh lives. . . ."

Why is it that complacent lies are always so
safe, and the truth is so dangerous? In our
meetings and retreats, we sit around in cozy
circles and nod to each other, affirming each
other's platitudes, while deep down in the
heart of many there is some cry, some
hunger, some fresh word from God so alive it
is washed with hot tears . . . but it seems that
there sit the other four hundred, nodding to
each other like wooden puppets and we are
choked with fear lest we awaken them and
they devour us.

As Yahweh lives, so will I. And as I dare to
live, so will God come alive in me.

"Daily I counter their malice with prayer."
Psalm 141:6

35

OUR LIVES ARE filled with a host of negative influences. We may be angry at people who have done us real or imagined wrongs. We may be burning with the fire of wanting things, and raw with the impatience of achieving goals. When we pray, these may be the things uppermost in our minds.

Yet if I ask God to get even with my enemies, to give me what I want, and to hasten the achievement of my lagging goals, the words of my prayer sound curiously flat, as though I am talking to myself. It is more of the same old thing, and utterly depressing. But if I raise my heart and spirit to center them on God, and let the flow of his love pass through me, cleansing me of my anger and wanting and impatience, I am renewed and refreshed. Prayer is exciting, I am released, and the malice is gone.

"No passover like this had ever been celebrated."
2 Kings 23:22

WE DO NOT very often link the words *confession* and *celebration* in our minds, but they have a definite correlation. Until I can clear my mind of the old, the downward, the heavy, the cloying, I am not free to soar and laugh and do a dance of joy in the presence of God.

If I am tied down with old grudges, I do not celebrate. I walk the streets making up hateful replies and figuring out how to squelch my opponent with that last killing word. If I find it hard to forgive, I am not free to be joyful, because I go about justifying in my mind why I should not forgive . . . that if such things are forgiven, the whole world will go to rack and ruin, and there will be no sense of justice left. But if I can knock down all the old idols of grudge and unforgiveness I have been defending in the name of righteousness, I will experience a sweeping sense of freedom. I will be free to *celebrate God!*

"Every face turned toward him grows brighter."
Psalm 34:5

37

THERE ARE SOME DAYS when I cannot pretend
that I feel great. A cold in the head, a poor
night's sleep, a disturbing letter from a
friend. . . . Goodness knows I have reason to
look like the bottom of the barrel!

But given *these rather grey circumstances,* I
still have one choice. I can lift my head and
look toward God, the source of light, or I can
turn my face and look the other way. If I
choose to look upward, my face can reflect
confidence, warmth, and a glow that does
not originate with me. Every face turned
toward him grows brighter . . . at least
brighter than it was!

38

A *WISE* PERSON may be stereotyped as someone so shrewd he is to be feared. He is the one who knows every angle of the game. He is a fighter. He has no time in his hectic schedule to be kind or considerate unless the other person is on his level of intellect . . . and deep compassion has no place in this image of the scholar or specialist.

But wisdom is a state of mind and spirit, not a condition we can study or earn ourselves into. The truly *wise* person, the person who has attached himself to the source of all wisdom, knows that any knowledge he accrues which takes him away from that source is not wise . . . only pseudo-wise; and being connected to that eternal source, he becomes a fountain of peace, of kindness, and consideration for others. Since his wisdom is not only of the head but also of the heart, he becomes the most compassionate of human beings. This is wisdom with a difference . . . God-wisdom.

*"His searching gaze scans all mankind
. . . upright men will contemplate his
face."*
Psalm 11:4, 7

39

As I GO about the streets and roads of my life,
it is interesting to think of watching God's
face as he sees the world I see. The good, the
evil, the questionable, the right, and
wrong. . . . And as I watch the lights and
shadows flicker across the face of God, I
realize it is not only for the actions of others
that I feel concern. I am one of the mass of
human beings he is watching, and the good,
the evil, the questionable, the right, and the
wrong all pass through the middle of me. I
am a part of what is happening.

Watching God's face as he gazes at the
world. . . . Somehow that helps me to be a
more sensitive, responsible person.

"To Yahweh belong the earth and all it holds, the world and all who live in it."
Psalm 24:1

THE WORLD BELONGS to God. This concept is the firm foothold of an integrated life. It gives one a sense of wholeness, a feeling of solidarity with the earth. And yet we see so much brokenness, so much fragmentation and disintegration. How do we account for this, if God is king?

There is a definition of wholeness in the Psalms, a description of one who is fit to appear before the king. "He whose hands are clean, whose heart is pure, and whose soul does not pay homage to worthless things. . . ." There are not too many of us who could be so defined. Perhaps what is in question is not God's kingship but our citizenship. Do my hands, heart, soul, and the value of my pursuits add anything to the wholeness of this world, God's world?

*"Let me sing to Yahweh for the
goodness he has shown me."*
Psalm 13:5

41

THERE ARE DAYS when the complexity of our
problems, the regrets for the past, the
gnawing fears for the future, and the worry
about responsibilities all play a dark game in
our minds. When we come to the end of the
day, we feel exhausted, beaten, and
defeated. The only remedy seems to be to go
to sleep and, hopefully, do better tomorrow.

But how? The problems are still there!
Perhaps a simple shift in my mind is all that is
needed. I will sing in my heart to God for the
goodness he has shown me, and in the
feeling of gratitude that comes, I will find new
perspectives. I will be warmed and opened.
God's power can flow through me to find
new solutions and cast out useless fears. I will
sing in my heart to God, and good things will
happen!

*"In my prosperity, I used to say,
'Nothing can ever shake me.'"*
Psalm 30:6

42

LIFE IS A curious mixture of light and
darkness, and no person, no matter how
strong, is without one weak point. Just when
we are feeling strongest the weak point can
give way, threatening to collapse the whole
structure of life.

If I know my weak points—the points I do
not understand about myself—and try to
understand them, will it help? I'm not sure.
Not until life applies genuine pressure to me
can I be tested. And then the test is this; does
the power of God in me have the strength to
mend this weakness? The answer to *that*
question is always YES!

"Not to go slandering other people or picking quarrels, but to be courteous and always polite to all kinds of people."
Titus 3:2

43

WHEN I FEEL insecure and disconnected from God, I tend to go around looking for faults in others. I dislike them for being richer or poorer, older or younger, having more or less than I do. I am the standard of all judgment (in the absence of any other God), and since there is no one else quite like me, everyone else is out of line.

But when my connection to God is real and vital, I am aware of the value of all life. I look less at who people are superficially—what they have, how they dress, what their lifestyle is—and look more to the center of the person. There, I usually find someone with whom I can identify. There is no necessity to put on a veneer of politeness over my true feelings. This person before me is a part of all life, an interconnected part of *my* life, and I give him my true respect. We have both come from God.

"So, since the law has no more than a reflection of these realities, and no finished picture of them, it is quite incapable of bringing the worshippers to perfection."
Hebrews 10:1

I SHOULD DO this, and you *should* do that, but both of us know that unless we *want* to, neither of us *will.*

For centuries men and women have known what they should do. These shoulds were written into laws, and people felt a sense of guilt when the laws were not kept. These laws did not produce motivation, they only produced guilt.

But when Christ came, he understood that men and women would not follow what they should, they would follow what they loved. By his simple, direct, piercing words, he probed to the hearts of people, and moved them to such love that the laws seemed shallow by comparison. What before had seemed compulsory was now not enough. For love, people would do more than they should!

*"Turn me from the path of delusion,
grant me the grace of your Law. I run
the way of your commandments, since
you have set me free."*
Psalm 119:29, 32

45

THERE ARE A hundred and one ways to get lost
in this world, and most of them start out
sounding like a good idea. But the paths to
most carefully avoid are the ones which claim
to be a shortcut or a bargain. A life worth
living is never obtained cheaply. It is a long
hard struggle.

These are questions I ask myself when trying
to make a decision which way to go. In spite
of what this would cost me, does it have
solidarity and depth? Is it exciting? Do I feel
an inner motivation to fight for it? Is it
creative, uplifting, positive, and deeply
satisfying? In spite of the hard work it will
cost me, will it make me feel freer? Will it
create for me the kind of life I want to live?
Will it make me be the kind of person I want
to be? The kind of person God wants me to
be?

If the answer to all these questions is yes,
then I will know I'm on the right road—the
road that will let me work hard for a life that
is worth everything I put into it.

"He asked for life and you gave it to him. . . . you gladden him with the joy of your presence."
Psalm 21:4, 6

46

THERE IS NOTHING worse than to live with a feeling of deadness, to awake and experience heaviness and despair. When such feelings overtake us, there is a great antidote.

I can begin at the bottom; thank God that I am alive, that all the millions of parts and pieces in my body and mind are functioning . . . and on top of this miracle the wonder of the human spirit, the presence of human personality and consciousness, the sense of worth and immortality. One might even say that a full self-consciousness is the beginning of God-consciousness, that the joy of being a person is the joy of recognizing the source of all life . . . in my one life.

"You are a king who loves justice, insisting on honesty, justice, and virtue."
Psalm 99:4

47

THE TRIANGLE OF honesty, justice, and virtue can build a life in which every angle is supported and strengthened by the other.

Honesty is basically my relationship with God. I am in so much danger of being dishonest with myself, that only in the clear light of God can I detect my own flaws and deceptions.

Justice has to do with the way I relate to those around me. It includes words like respect, fairness, responsibility, reliability, promises and commitments. Justice is my people-angle.

And virtue, that word which cuts so close we tend to laugh about it, centers on our inner selves. It touches what we love, what we want. It probes our longings, our leanings, our ability to square what we are with what we would be. It calls us to shape up, to look up, to be honest. . . . Honest? We are back to where we started from, with God.

"They refused a land of delight . . .
they stayed . . . and grumbled."
Psalm 106:24

48

THE LAND OF delight always seems just over
the next hill and around the bend. It is
usually a little farther than we had thought.
The temptation is to give up, to complain
about tired feet and jaded dreams and how
unfair it all is . . . and to sit by the road and
grumble about what fools other people are to
chase the rainbow.

But if I can draw on God for courage to push
ahead with plans and goals, I will be able to
move toward all the excitement life has in
store for me. People who give up have
nothing to do but grumble, and they quickly
become lifeless and bitter. What a thing to
trade for that sweet sense of adventure!

"He sees himself with too flattering an eye to detect and detest his guilt."
Psalm 36:2

49

THE POWER OF GOD is not a magic panacea to get me out of situations which I have stumbled into by being destructive. Whenever I begin to claim that I am the innocent victim of circumstances, I hesitate; for into the scale of my mind there begins to pour a pile of small deceits and grains of arrogance that I have tossed into the balance, a pinch of pride, and a little gloating, along with the idea that I was quite shrewd and savvy. . . . When the scale comes down to my disfavor, do I have the right to pose as the innocent victim and to ask for divine help?

Hardly. The only right I have is to pour out the whole unvarnished truth and ask for forgiveness, both from God and from the person I have offended. When the obstructions are removed, then God's power can flow through me again.

*"Never let the sun set on your anger,
or else you will give the devil a
foothold."*
Ephesians 4:26–27

ANGER IS A normal, healthy reaction. It springs
up in me when I feel I have been wronged,
or snubbed, or taken advantage of. Anger in
itself is not wrong. It is as natural as sneezing
when dust gets in one's nose.

But unchanneled anger, anger which sits and
rankles in my mind, can be destructive.
Repressed anger saps my energy and
paralyzes my spirit; and in the vacuum
created by inaction, the slow process of
self-destruction can set in. I have been
wronged, therefore I have the right to be
cross, overeat, overdrink, be moody—

What can I do when I am angry? Turn to the
source of the anger, and take some positive
action to alleviate the cause. Kicking the cat
or eating a hot fudge sundae will not help.

"There are all sorts of service to be done, but always to the same Lord; working in all sorts of different ways in different people, it is the same God who is working in all of them."
1 Corinthians 12:5–7

AT TIMES my concept of God gets so narrow that I get bored with it myself. Then I know that I have short-changed the Spirit of the eternal God!

The person who would serve God in this world does not need to be doing something overtly religious; rather, the Spirit of God can be thought of as a connecting thread which strings together all the activities of life, giving them continuity and order.

Am I carrying on a conversation with a stranger? The Spirit in me recognizes the stranger as a friend. Am I relating to a family member? God in me recognizes the family member as a valid person. If God's Spirit is in me, acknowledged and strong in my consciousness, whatever I wear, eat, drink, say . . . wherever I go, I will have a sense of purpose. The Spirit of God is the hidden shape that in-forms my life.

"Our Lord is great, all-powerful, of infinite understanding."
Psalm 147:5

IN EVERY IDEAL there is a skillful blending of opposites. God the creator is all-powerful, and when persons or nations or human processes are slow in their development, he in his power could strike them dead in a moment, totally impatient with their blundering and wandering ways. But this total power has the check and balance of total understanding, understanding *why* persons and nations and human institutions have such a struggle in their development. He has infinite patience with them. He will not quickly use the power to destroy because his nature is to create.

This balance must be mine, if I am to be a conscious part of God's creative process. The more power I am given, the more understanding I must be.

*"But after a while the stream dried up,
for the country had no rain. And then
the word of Yahweh came to him,
'Up, and go. . . .'"*
1 Kings 17:7

GOD HAD ORDERED Elijah to go to the stream
and live there. The orders were sharp and
clear, and Elijah had no doubts. But the day
came when the stream dried up. How
discouraged the prophet must have felt! Had
he been mistaken to come to this place? Was
God forsaking him?

Neither of these fears proved true. Elijah had
been right in coming, but now that the
stream was dry, he was justified in going.
God did not expect him to sit beside a dry
streambed and blindly obey yesterday's
orders.

We may not be prophets, but we are all
people who have to be ready to hear the
words, "Up, and go. The stream is dry
here."

> *"Jereboam thought to himself, 'As things are, the kingdom will revert to the house of David. If this people continue to go up to the Temple of Yahweh in Jerusalem to offer sacrifices, the people's heart will turn back again to . . . the king of Judah, and they will put me to death.'"*
> 1 Kings 12:26–27

IF GOD IS LOVE, then fear must be the devil. Fear makes us do strange things. We may have a dream in mind, a goal, a relationship, a friendship . . . and then set out to accomplish it by doing everything that will guarantee its destruction. Fear makes us destroy what we love most.

I do not need to act out of fear. If I love another person, I do not need to build a fence around him or her in a grasping way. If I love life, I will not need to suffer through the present as I strain toward a doubtful future. If I love God, I will know that what I am right now is all right, and that anything else I become will be a gift. Secure futures are built up one day at a time, out of todays that are sufficient in themselves in the love of God. Fear only breeds disaster.

"He was a highly intelligent craftsman, skilled in all types of bronzework. He came to King Solomon and did all this work for him."
1 Kings 7:14

55

MOST OF US are caught in the web of survival from sunup to sundown. We grow up and establish families. We work and nourish and parent and feed. There arise among us men and women whose lives are unusual, skilled, whose talent and gift for creating beauty stirs within us a longing to express, to do something that will outlast us . . . but we are caught in the web and have no time.

No time? We have each been given twenty-four hours in a day, and much of it is spent in non-productive activities—activities that are not even especially pleasant, but merely pass the time. Time will pass fast enough on its own. If there is in us a buried longing to create something beautiful . . . if the voice of the Creator is calling to us from within . . . take the time. Take a few moments of the day to create something that will outlive the span of your years, and you will know what it is to be part of the Eternal.

"The man who puts on his armour is not the one who can boast, but the man who takes it off."
1 Kings 20:11

TO BEGIN A PROJECT is within the power of almost anyone, but the beginning of a project is a very poor time to boast about its success. Between the intention and the completion of any task there lie a hundred pitfalls, with the danger of failure always hovering in the background to keep us humble. Not until the battle is over do we know if we have succeeded or failed.

I hope that someday God gives me the wisdom not to be the one who shouts while I am putting on my armor, but to be the one who can breathe a prayer of thanks when I take it off . . . and discover I am still alive.

"'Your request is a difficult one,'
Elijah said. 'If you see me while I am
being taken from you, it shall be as
you ask; if not, it will not be so.'"
2 Kings 2:10

THE STRENGTH of our faith is possible only in relationship to what we have seen and lived through. Others, older and wiser, may wish to give us a portion of their spirit, but it is not theirs to give.

A perceptive spirit is not like a will that can be written out and passed on. As much as we long for the strength and spirit of others to be ours, it cannot happen by simply wishing it to be so. The younger and the older must walk together to the end of the road, like Elisha and the old prophet. We may doubt, all during the journey, that we will ever be the possessors of the faith of our fathers. Yet somehow in the experience of their passing we know that the mantle has fallen to us, that we are now the carriers of that fire, and that those who are younger will look to us. In that experience we are infused with a spirit that never leaves us . . . and the presence of that Spirit transforms our lives.

"Pause a while and know that I am God."
Psalm 46:10

IN THE JUMBLED, hectic events of a day, most of us are vaguely aware that there is a God somewhere; and although we may not feel that he is doing a very good job in some areas, we dimly hope that he is there—that someone is in control. We may not even want to think about it at all, to repress the fear that the world is careening through space like a bus without a driver.

But a moment's pause can make a tremendous difference. If I can close my eyes and think past the jumbled whirl of people and events, back past the world as it now is, back to the point of man's origin, and even farther than that to the beginning of life, the first living cell . . . the mystery of life . . . the intelligence that must be there . . . the overwhelming intelligence that must guide the motions of this complex universe. . . . Perhaps I can trust my world to this God.

"Spend your night in quiet meditation."
Psalm 4:4

"Yahweh works wonders for those He loves."
Psalm 4:3

THERE ARE MANY kinds of nights. A night is not always the section of a twenty-four hour day that we usually consign to darkness; it can be the night of the spirit . . . a time when things seem black around us, when it is impossible to see where we are going, when a feeling of tiredness and heaviness closes in around us. . . .

During such nights, it is good to spend time in meditation, letting one's muddy waters settle, letting the power of God flow through, asking nothing, wanting nothing, waiting, accepting.

God works wonders for those he loves. Morning will come.

"You hope for light, but he will turn it into deep shadow. . . . If you do not listen."
Jeremiah 13:16–17

THE HOPE FOR a bright future is a dream that is planted in every healthy human mind. Perhaps it is the little shadow of heaven that we are all born with. . . .

But how we plan those futures will dictate whether the days ahead will turn into a bit of heaven or a lot of hell. As I look down the road to my tomorrows, am I including God in my plans? Am I willing to acknowledge that he will be there, all-seeing, all-knowing, all-judging? The motivations I have at this moment will be magnified a thousand times as I live them. God will be there. Will he fit, or will I have to suppress my God-consciousness in order to succeed?

God will be there, and long beyond *my* life he will remain the source of all true creativity and strength. If my future is built on this awareness, it will be bright.

"God, I have made a new song for you. . . ."
Psalm 144:9

61

THERE ARE DAYS, in every household, when things get all scrambled up. The car has a dent in it, someone has forgotten to feed the dog, there is ink on the living room furniture, parents seem unreasonable, and children seem irresponsible. The air is filled with tension: with fussing, complaining, nagging, criticism, sharp words, and anger all rising like a dissonant howl.

Then someone has the courage to say, "STOP. This must not be!" We need a new song, a remembering of good things, a listing of dreams, a change of horizons. One warm word, a kind smile, a hug, and the world is changed. The ink, the dog, the car, and the growing-up traumas are all still there, but the score has changed. We are singing a new song, a God-song, a love song.

"Religion . . . does bring large profits, but only to those who are content with what they have."
1 Timothy 6:6

IF I AM NOT content with what I have, everything I get seems to fall into a large, hungry, greedy hole. Nothing is ever enough. I need more. . . .

Jesus Christ told us that contentment does not come from the number of things we possess. His formula for contentment was to love God with all the heart, and one's neighbor as oneself, to even go beyond the words of love to the extent of caring for and suffering with people. He taught us to enjoy each day as it comes, and to live it gratefully, always stretching toward new understanding and a larger spirit. The profits that come from living this kind of a life are bound to be so enormous that we will hardly be able to contain them, and may find ourselves spilling over, with plenty to share. There is enough, so much more than we need.

"My master has let this [man] off lightly, by not accepting what he offered. . . . I will run after him and get something out of him."
2 Kings 5:20

I WILL GET *something out of him* . . . these are dangerous words. If I ever stoop to think them, I may be sure that something in me will instinctively cloak them in the brightest of smiles, in the thickest of courtesy, in undivided attention toward the one who is to be *had.* These words are the basis of a poisonous relationship.

I may be sure, also, that even while I am fawning, smiling, scraping, and bowing before my victim, I will end up getting more than I asked for. Along with the favor I seek I will be given the gifts of self-disgust, emptiness, and chagrin. Wanting to get something out of other people is the surest way of destroying myself.

"Your zeal has been a spur to many more."
2 Corinthians 9:3

HOW EXCITING IT IS to say to a friend who is doubting himself, "Try it! You can do it!" and then to see that friend succeed. It is almost better than having to go through the pangs of success oneself.

There is adventure in encouraging others, but the true test of our enthusiasm for life is whether or not we can remain full of that enthusiasm ourselves in the daily round of existence. What do others think of when they see my name? Do they think of a person whose enthusiasm is bubbling and contagious, or a person whose lethargy is a drag? Nobody loves a drag, and I would suspect that even God—that bubbling, leaping, surging force of life—finds it hard to live in one so out of character with himself.

*"Jeremiah then took another scroll
and gave it to the scribe."*
Jeremiah 36:32

JEREMIAH WAS A stubborn old prophet who refused to take no for an answer. When all that he had dreamed of saying went up in flames, he simply started over again. What he had to say, in the name of God, was going to be said.

Fortunate is the person who has such a clear sense of his mission in this world. The person who is caught up in doing what is important to him does not fear danger, ridicule, disappointment, setbacks, or apparent disfavor. His motivation does not stem from immediate success or recognition, but from a deep conviction within. In the strength of this conviction, he can forge ahead when there is not a single sign that he will ever meet with acclaim. His determination does not come from a shallow source that is here today and gone tomorrow, but from a deep spring within.

It is amazing how many of these men and women have counted in the progress of the world.

*"I am with you to save you . . . I will
not make an end of you, only
discipline you in moderation, so as not
to let you go. . . ."*
Jeremiah 30:11

A STRONG CONNECTION with the power of God
does not always produce a smooth, peaceful
life. When a human being realizes the
potential that is his or hers by being a
container of this mighty power, this person
expects much of himself. Nothing but the
highest character code will do. Nothing but
the fairest judgments are right. Nothing but
the most excellent work is good enough.
Nothing can be done in a careless manner,
because everything matters very much. . . .

Yet to keep from being overdisciplined to the
point where one becomes rigid and
unfeeling, this life has a built-in safeguard.
The only thing that *supremely* matters is the
heart of God himself, which is love.

"In all this misfortune, Job uttered no sinful word."
Job 2:10

67

THERE ARE TIMES when I feel justified in losing my calm, times when I can tolerate no more, and my only response is black, explosive, undirected anger. . . .

Undirected? Not quite. Once I give in to this response, I realize how pointless it is, that any genuine strength which comes to me will come in the silent, private rearrangement of my priorities, in resorting to my inner strengths. For when I lose control and curse life, I only curse that portion of God's power which lives in me, and ultimately, curse the core of my self.

*"You will need endurance to do God's
will and gain what He has promised."*
Hebrews 10:36

GOD IS ETERNAL. To do God's will is not a
single act that one accomplishes and then it is
done. God's will is a state of *being,* as lasting
as life itself. It is a state of *doing.*

God's will is not a fixed thing. In the twistings
and turnings of life, it is sometimes to the
right, sometimes to the left, sometimes
above, sometimes below. While life bobs
about like the water from a leaping fountain,
that core of "what God will have done" stays
steady, yet flexible.

But what is God's will? If I can think of all the
things that God is—love, justice, mercy,
honesty—I can know that his will would be
the active state of all these. And if my will is
in tune with the eternal will, I will have the
endurance I need to keep on doing. When I
understand that God's will is eternal, I stop
trying to accomplish it by Friday.

*"The only purpose of this instruction is
that there should be love, coming out
of a pure heart, a clear conscience and
a sincere faith."*
1 Timothy 1:5

ALL MY BELIEVING, all my seeking after God,
my wanting to be in the flow of his
power—what is the end purpose of it? How
can I tell when my life is operating properly,
when I am in line?

These are indicators: When my life is guided
by the motivating force of love, not loves that
are possessive or manipulative or
domineering, but love that flows out of a
heart that is open and without duplicity.
When I have a conscience that is clear, even
in the middle of the darkest night. When my
faith in God is so sincere it is almost
instinctive. When I keep on believing in the
triumph of goodness even when the worst
forces in the world seem to be winning, and
can go on being sincere even when it is a
laugh-word. . . . Then I can relax and know
that my faith is serving its true purpose.

"The heart of Asa was wholly with Yahweh throughout his life."
1 Kings 15:14

70

IT IS A beautiful thing to live a day, feeling the heart of God beating in my heart. The whole world takes on a sense of wonder and awe. The first moment of consciousness is like a rush of love and welcome. The coffee smells good. The bacon has a great fragrance. I feel as though I am bursting with life and could conquer worlds.

During the day, people seem more wonderful. I can feel their hearts, beating with my heart and the great heart of God. Their joys are like mine, and their sorrows hurt all of us. What is mine and what is theirs does not seem so sharply divided, because it all belongs to something beyond us and is only loaned to us.

And at night, when I lie down to rest, there is a rush of gratitude. I am not alone, for my life is bigger than my one self. I am a part of the great God-heart.

". . . you have an ambition that you cannot satisfy; so you fight to get your way by force."
James 4:2

71

THERE IS A fine line between being deeply dedicated to accomplish and being driven by greedy ambition. The only way one can tell the difference is to look ahead to the final objective. What is the reward that impels me to fight on?

There are two deep motivations that are common to mankind. One arises out of the desire for power, proved by the possession of things; the other stems from the desire for meaning, validated by purposeful contributions to life. If two people driven by these two motivations are put side by side, a difference can be observed in their actions. The one who is goaded to power by the acquisition of things knows no limit to the means he will employ to reach his goals. . . . But the person who is motivated by meaning has a built-in censor. If he stoops to meanness or violence in his battle to achieve his goal, it is already lost.

If I must fight and get my way by force, perhaps I should look ahead and see what it is that I am fighting for.

72

As PERSONS WHO are filled with the spirit of God, we are by nature avid seekers of truth. This seeking is not one that must take us on long journeys in search of magic revelations or formulas, but makes us seekers of what is true for us each day in our work and relationships.

To identify with God, who does not lie, gives me a certain kind of character. It makes me keen to search out the truth and side with it, or else to sense that truth has many sides and to encompass them all in my understanding. But most of all, being a seeker of truth means striking for the heart of what is genuine, touching the living core of every conversation, transaction, or piece of work. The truth is the essence of each matter, and all the rest is a waste of life.

*"The Lord gave it to me for building
you up and not for pulling you down."*
2 Corinthians 10:8

THE PEOPLE we live with every day can
become the objects of our most gross
insensitivity. To the world outside, we must
be positive, charming, interesting, helpful,
and cooperative, if we hope to succeed. But
with the people who are already ours, we
dare to be negative, boring, dull, selfish, and
rude. We do not mean to be. . . . It is simply
the fact that familiarity breeds blindness.

We have been given to each other to build
each other up. Just because I love you and
we have known each other for years, I do not
have the right to tell you that you are being
stupid when you already know you are being
less than your best. I have the privilege of
reminding you how brilliant you really are
and of helping you to see that your present
slump is totally out of character with your
real self, which is actually marvelous.
Because you belong to me, I am close
enough to take the pieces of you which have
fallen apart, temporarily, and help you build
again. I never have the right to take you
apart.

"Live a life worthy of God, who is calling to you to share the glory of his kingdom."
1 Thessalonians 2:12

74

THE FLOW of God's power reaches toward me each day, each morning. It calls me to put up my hands and welcome it, to set myself in line with its flow, to open my being to its glow.

But I can refuse. I can crouch down and hide from the light and joy streaming toward me. I can refuse to let it enter me. Yet . . . how can I resist? When I stop to listen, there is that voice, calling me, inviting me to share in light and power and warmth. As a product of the master creator, my life is worth too much to turn away and crouch in the dark. I am a part of God. It is only when I turn away from the light that I feel the darkness is winning.

"Yahweh . . . bring us back, let your
face smile on us and we shall be safe."
Psalm 80:19

75

To A CROWD of people going down a street,
that same street can be many things. It can
be a joyful place, a fearsome place, a
loathsome place, or a place of great
adventure. It will be what each person
perceives it to be.

How do we perceive the streets of our lives?
It is true, there are dangers wherever we go.
Life has a dark element. In every living thing
there lurks the seed of death, and in every
opportunity there is danger. How can a
person ever have a feeling of safety in this
world? It sounds impractical, and perhaps
only those who dare to experience it know
what it is . . . but the feeling that God *is,* the
faith that creation will have the last word over
destruction, this is the safe feeling that God is
smiling on his world. It must sometimes be a
tongue-in-cheek smile, but a smile
nonetheless.

"I would lay down my life at any moment. . . ."
Psalm 119:109

76

Is THERE ANYTHING that I love enough to die for? If so, it's probably the same as the thing I'm living for. Only things and persons who command our deepest love are worth living or dying for.

A husband, a wife, a friend, a child. . . . When I say I would die for someone, I am saying that they inspire in me the intense desire to live. They give life meaning at such depth that the meaning transcends life itself.

And what earthly tie can we make that will be this lasting? In the end we come back to ourselves and the God-within, who is our reason for living. He will be our reason for dying, and it will all be the same love that moves us.

> *"Try to discover what the Lord wants of you, having nothing to do with the futile works of darkness, but exposing them by contrast."*
> *Ephesians 5:10–11*

SOMETIMES IT IS difficult to know what God wants me to do . . . and at other times I know I simply use this statement as a religious cop-out for not knowing my own mind. What do *I* want to do?

Asking myself what I really want to do is perhaps the best test of whether or not my life is centered in God. Could I take what I would truly desire most and hold it up before God to ask for his presence and power to make it possible? Can I take my dreams, ambitions, plans, and schemes and lay them out before God, asking his blessing . . . or do I have to suppress the things I want most in order to follow what I think God would like? Until my own deepest wishes square with what God would wish for me, I will never be a strongly integrated person. *God has made me, and his clearest purpose for me is that I be my own best self.*

"I do not claim one extra bull from your homes. . . . No, let thanksgiving be your sacrifice. . . . What business have you reciting my statutes? . . . You are leaving God out of account; take care."

Psalm 50:9, 14, 16, 22

78

LIFE IS NOT to be composed basically of doing the right things, giving the right amounts, saying the right words, keeping up all the right appearances . . . but of a heart attitude made up of deep integrity, and a goodness that is so ingrained and stubborn it cannot be corrupted at any price. The quoting of Scripture should come out of a heart that says, "I know that's true, I've experienced it!" and not out of a mouth that says, "Yes, I know I should be like that, but I can't be . . . and God forgives."

*"If anyone wants to boast, let him
boast of this: of understanding and
knowing me. For I . . . rule with
kindness, justice and integrity on
earth."*
Jeremiah 9:24

79

ANYTHING THAT I pride myself on being or
knowing can, if I am not careful, pull me off
center and destroy my sense of being
well-integrated. Most of my sources of pride
contain the seeds of their own disintegration.
If I boast of being wise, my greatest fear will
be of being seen as foolish. If I boast of being
strong, I will be terrified by my own
weaknesses. If I boast of what I possess,
nothing will strike horror in me so deeply as
the thought of losing those possessions.

But what if my main claim to worth is that I
belong to God? What a different set of
pressures this puts on me! Since God is
kindness, I am obligated to deal in kindness,
and since he is justice and integrity, my main
fears become associated with losing my sense
of justice toward others and becoming
deceitful within. These pressures will never
destroy me, but always pull me toward
center.

*"If Yahweh does not build the house,
in vain the masons toil."*
Psalm 127:1

THE MOTIONS that we go through in the
process of living either have meaning for us,
or we find ourselves mired in total futility.
Most of life is spent in going through
routines.

I can get up in the morning, a little miffed at
the indignity of having to wake up. I can eat
breakfast, wondering why I have to eat the
same thing every morning. I can go to school
or to work or to the grocery store, caught in a
hopeless sense of the dullness of life. I can do
this, if I choose. . . .

Or I can wake up with a feeling of energy
inside me, grateful for a new day, a new
chance to work and feel alive . . . a new
opportunity to say, "I love you" to someone
important. I can eat whatever food there is
with a sense of gratitude in a world where so
many are hungry. I can go to school or to
work or to the store, ready for some new
adventure . . . or perhaps open to see
something I've never seen before. If I
recognize that God is building my life, even
in its routines, this is the choice I will make.

"Man when he prospers forfeits intelligence: he is one with the cattle doomed to slaughter."
Psalm 49:12

AN ANIMAL being fattened becomes placid. Its survival instincts are dulled. It may feel that life has never been so good, when actually it is being prepared for slaughter.

There is always the danger that we may become one of the unthinking herd. In the frantic scramble for possessions and security, our minds may become dulled to what we know is important in life. Money itself is not evil, but the pressure to have it can blur our sense of equality and justice. When I have money in the bank and in my pocket, I need to think more clearly than ever in order to keep my priorities straight so I will not become one of the mindless herd being blandly pushed toward my own destruction.

*"How many wonders you have done
for us, Yahweh . . . how many plans
you have made for us."*
Psalm 40:5

IT SEEMS cliché to say that God has plans for
us. Is it modesty, or pride, or a sense of
wanting to find our own way that makes us
smile at the idea that God the Almighty has
plans for our lives?

Yet as we glance back over the stumbling
and bumbling of our unsure steps, the
failures, and almost accidental successes,
there appears to be a pattern—a
progression. God has led, and the pattern
has been consistent. If at each turn of the
road we choose what is highest, most
creative, most integrated, and most whole,
somehow mysteriously we find that God has
been leading us.

*"Yahweh gave, Yahweh has taken
back."*
Job 1:21

GOD GIVES TO each of us a life to celebrate,
and when it is over, he takes us back to
himself.

What does it mean to be ready to die? A life
that has been celebrated to the full, one that
has known happiness and goodness and
hard work and rough times . . . and the joy of
overcoming hardship and laughing in the
face of adversity. . . . What can the passing of
such a life be but another celebration? It is
only sad to die when we have *not* taken the
life God gave us and given it back to him in
joyful service. It is one of life's ironies that we
weep most desolately when the unfulfilled
die, and taste no bitterness in our sorrow
when we grieve for a life that has been of
great service. Perhaps we are never ready to
die until we have learned to live.

*"How unreliable these people who
refuse to grasp my ways!"*
Hebrews 3:11

84

GOD'S WAYS always take us by surprise. It is
not that we refuse to grasp them so much as
that they sneak up on us and astound us.

In the beginning of a venture, we usually
have a strong feeling that it is right. The
project is begun with high enthusiasm. Then
difficulties are encountered and disillusionment sets in. With the disillusionment comes
doubt that this was the right thing to do, and
there is the suspicion that we have somehow
been deluded. There are moments of
meaning, but then comes the breaking point
at which we know this particular venture is
over. We may feel sad, that we have
failed. . . . And then suddenly, as we stand
aside and look at the whole experience, there
is a flood of understanding . . . not the
understanding we were searching for, but a
whole new world.

"Well you know, Yahweh, the course of man is not in his control, nor is it in man's power . . . to guide his steps. Correct us, Yahweh, gently. . . ."
Jeremiah 10:23–24

LIFE IS A puzzling balance between finding our own way and recognizing that in some mysterious fashion God is leading us. We know that we must be thinking people who make responsible decisions, and yet sometimes when we look back, God has led us in ways that never entered our imagination at the time!

How does it work, this balance between hard-headed common sense and the leading of the spirit of God? Very delicately! I need to be aware that the life of God is in me and make the best decisions at every turn of the road. I have to be honest about what my gifts are and what is right for me. Outward appearances cannot be primary, but rather the inner growth and health of all who will be affected by the decision. If these are my guidelines, I will be free to choose so wisely that God himself could hardly have made a better choice for me.

*"Whatever work you propose to do,
do it while you can."*
Ecclesiastes 9:10

PLANNING WHAT I will do someday is an idle
dream. Someday I will travel, will paint, will
write, will start a neighborhood group, will
spend more time with my children, will do
something kind for my parents, will start a
keep-fit program. Someday, I am going to be
a terrific person. The problem is that
someday never comes. It is even more
elusive than tomorrow.

Many years of our lives are spent in
maturing, and even more years in training.
We grow accustomed to waiting. But then
the day arrives when we are *there,* an adult,
in the heart of our productive years. What do
we propose to do in life? Is it to be one
specialized drive, or a series of events leading
to a cohesive purpose? One thing is sure.
Whatever we propose to do, this is the time.
These are the days.

"It was by faith that . . . he held to his purpose like a man who could see the Invisible."
Hebrews 11:27

87

SOME OF THE greatest goals in life are the hardest to define. If someone had given a piece of paper to Einstein or Michaelangelo or Copernicus at the age of sixteen, and asked him to write on it what he hoped to contribute to the world, he might have been at a complete loss.

And with some of us, it lasts long past sixteen! We take jobs in order to survive. We raise families and go through all the socially acceptable outward forms of life. But still, burning under these things there may be a hidden dream, a deep desire to move toward a goal which has not yet been achieved, perhaps never yet been defined. As long as we have life we can still cling to our own unique dream, as men and women who can see that which is not yet visible to anyone else.

*"May he give you power through his
spirit for your hidden self to grow
strong. . . ."*
Ephesians 3:16

EACH OF US is given an identity at birth. It is
good to affirm this identity, being grateful for
the strengths it has given, and forgiving the
weaknesses.

But each of us has another, a hidden
identity. God's power within gives us the
potential to be a unique expression of his life.
The seed of that uniqueness, deep inside,
can only grow as we burst old shells and
layers of identity. The sprouting seed, the
tentative shoot, the uncurling leaf, the fragile
blossom. . . . Who would forego the
excitement of these for the warm comfort of
remaining in the soil?

Accepting my identity is good, but
discovering my unique self is even better.
When I have blossomed on my own, I will
have something new to give back to the life
cycle.

IT IS HARDLY fair to decry tradition until we
have given it a fair chance. Whatever is
handed down to us in life should be accepted
and treated with respect . . . at least until we
have tried it. Tradition is a good point from
which to start our individual journeys.

But those who are full of the creative push of
God remember that life is always going
forward. If we sit in the mind of the past
where God was, we may miss the ongoing
rush of that Spirit in the present and in the
future. To the past we owe our respect. To
the present we owe our diligence, and to the
future we owe the best of our dreams. It is
always an overwhelming surprise to walk
toward our wildest imaginings, and find God
there with his hands stretched out to us . . .
and to realize he is expecting us. It is like a
great homecoming.

*"As your word unfolds, it gives light,
and the simple understand."*
Psalm 119:130

THE DAWNING of a new day is a mysterious experience that we all live through every twenty-four hours. The deep, dark, formless blackness . . . the streak of light, drawing a magical division between land and sky . . . the dim shapes of the city or the tops of trees . . . then gentle morning. By high noon, with the scene so bright one can hardly take it in, who can even remember what those same shapes looked like, wrapped in darkness?

Like a day dawning, our understanding of God unfolds, a little light at a time, so gently it is almost imperceptible. But when the fullness of that awareness comes, we will not even be able to recall the dark shapes of doubt that once shrouded our emerging spirits. At high noon, nothing casts a shadow.